SMOOTHIE
power

80 POWER PACKED
Smoothie Recipes
for Every Day and Everyone

Irina Pawassar &
Tanja Dusy

FAIR WINDS

Quarto is the authority on a wide range of topics.

Quarto educates, entertains and enriches the lives of
our readers—enthusiasts and lovers of hands-on living.

www.QuartoKnows.com

The content in this book was created from four previously published titles:
Smoothies—Power For You, Smoothies for Kids, and *Green Smoothies*
by Irina Pawassar; and *Smoothie Bowls* by Tanya Dusy.

First published in the United States of America in 2017 by
Fair Winds Press, an imprint of
Quarto Publishing Group USA Inc.
100 Cummings Center
Suite 406-L
Beverly, Massachusetts 01915-6101
Telephone: (978) 282-9590
Fax: (978) 283-2742
QuartoKnows.com
Visit our blogs at QuartoKnows.com

21 20 19 18 17   1 2 3 4 5

ISBN: 978-1-59233-769-9

Library of Congress Cataloging-in-Publication Data available

Design: Ilona Molnár and Leeloo Molnár
Photography: Brigitte Sporrer, pages 10–135; Klaus-Maria Einwanger, 136–177, 179; and
Erik Pawassar 178

Printed in China

The information in this book is for educational purposes only. It is not intended to replace the advice
of a physician or medical practitioner. Please se... ur health-care provider before beginning any

CONTENTS

Basics 4
Ingredients 6
Superfoods! 8

SMOOTHIES FOR YOU 10

GREEN SMOOTHIES 52

SMOOTHIES FOR KIDS 94

SMOOTHIE BOWLS 136

About the Authors ... 178
Index 180

BASICS

POWER IN 10 MINUTES

They're fun, powerful, keep you healthy, and provide a refreshing boost of energy. Smoothies are conquering the world, and once you develop a taste for them, you won't want to go without.

DONE IN A JIFFY

Smoothies are ideal for people who want to eat healthier but don't want to dramatically change their whole diet. With smoothies, you simply add what you like to the blender jar and blend it up! Then, pour your elixir into your favorite bottle or to-go cup, rinse out the blender, and you're all set to go! It can be done in as little as 10 minutes, which is ideal for busy mornings. It's the perfect breakfast, snack for the office, or simply a cool refreshment for a hot summer day.

WE ARE WHAT WE EAT!

Regularly consuming smoothies, especially greens, has sort of an "awakening" effect on the body. Your mind becomes clearer and your taste buds more sensitive. You will notice that you don't need as much sugar or salt as you previously did. This is the first step towards a conscious diet.

HEALTH AND VITALITY

Greens are essential! Chlorophyll is the pigment in green plants that absorbs light and gives them their green color. It has extremely positive effects on our health! Raw vegetables also provide us with important enzymes, which can promote cell building and renewal. The more of these enzymes we have in our bodies, the more resilient our immune systems become. Smoothies can help make us fit and provide us with increased energy and vitality.

THE EQUIPMENT

A standard household blender will suffice for most recipes. A heavy-duty immersion blender gets great results as well. The better your appliance, the finer the ingredients can be blended. For chopping kale, pumpkin, pomegranate seeds, and certain types of nuts, a high performance blender will be necessary. Experiment and find out what texture you prefer: nice and smooth or with little fruit chunks; thick and creamy or thin like juice. It's all a matter of taste.

THE BASIC RULES

Using seasonal and locally sourced ingredients is the key. The focus doesn't always have to be on exotic superfoods. This book includes recipes using readily available ingredients, but also features some more tropical recipes for those seasons when the local fruit and vegetable selections are a little slim. For variety and a little something extra, you can always add the powerful superfoods listed in the Ingredients section.

All the recipes are vegan, except if you're using honey as sweetener. If you prefer cow's milk or yogurt, those can be substituted instead of almond or rice milk or coconut yogurt. Ingredients like cane sugar, gluten, and soy are left out.

Organic origin for all the produce is preferable, but not necessary. Serving sizes for all recipes yield enough for one to two people but can be adjusted as needed.

The smoothie label Super Danke contributed some of the recipes. These are acknowledged by their logo.

STRAIGHT TALK

There are no more excuses not to do a little something for your health and have fun along the way!

INGREDIENTS

VEGETABLES: Fresh, local, and seasonal is the name of the game. Organic vegetables or ones from your garden are perfect. Vitamins, minerals, dietary fibers, and low calorie counts make vegetables the perfect slimming agent.

FRUITS: Fruits taste great, are healthy, and give the smoothies their sweetness. Besides important vitamins, minerals, and dietary fibers, fruits contain a large number of beneficial secondary plant substances. It is best if you buy ripe, local, and seasonal fruits. The riper the fruit, the less you will have to sweeten the smoothie.

HERBS: Plants contain chlorophyll, especially leafy greens and fresh herbs. It helps detoxify the body, protects the immune system, and is rich in antioxidants. The darker the green of the ingredient, the more chlorophyll it contains.

LIQUIDS: Water is the ideal liquid to use to thin out smoothies because it doesn't contribute any additional calories. Natural spring water and regular filtered water are the best choices. But other healthy and tasty alternatives are coconut water or almond or rice milk.

SWEETENER: Say goodbye to cane sugar! Sweeten your smoothies with coconut sugar, honey, maple syrup, xylitol, or a little stevia.

SPICES: Using spices, such as cardamom and vanilla, will give your smoothies an additional punch of flavor.

NUTS AND SEEDS: When shopping, buy whole nuts that you can grind yourself when needed. Nuts and seeds are rich in fat, dietary fibers, and protein. They're an important energy and nutrient source.

ALWAYS-WORKS-SUPER-CRUNCHY-GRANOLA

½ cup (80 g) almonds
3 cups (150 g) grains (i.e. 3-grain-, oat-, or spelt flakes)
3 tablespoons (25 g) sunflower seeds
3 tablespoons (25 g) sesame seeds
1½ tablespoons (25 g) hemp seeds
2 tablespoons (25 g) flax seeds
½ cup (30 g) coconut flakes
¼ teaspoon cinnamon
¼ teaspoon ground ginger
¼ teaspoon cardamom
4 tablespoons (85 g) honey or (80 g) maple syrup
3 tablespoons (45 g) sunflower oil
½ cup (50 g) dried cranberries or goji berries to taste

This recipe is not only super crunchy, but it is also super easy:

Preheat the oven to 350°F (180°C, or gas mark 4).

Using a knife, chop the almonds into rough pieces (halved or thirds is enough).

Mix the chopped almonds together with the grains, sunflower, hemp, and flax seeds, coconut flakes, and spices in a bowl. Add the honey or maple syrup and sunflower oil; mix well using a spoon or your hands until the mixture is all well coated.

Move the mixture to a parchment-lined baking sheet and use a spoon to evenly spread it out across the entire baking sheet. Bake for 20 to 25 minutes (on the middle rack), stirring occasionally, until everything is nicely browned.

Remove the baking sheet from oven and let the roasted granola cool completely. If needed, stir again so that it doesn't clump together (or just let it set if you like bigger pieces). Once cooled, stir in the dried fruit to taste and transfer to an airtight container.

REALLY COOL: Frozen fruits (especially berries) have not only the advantage of always being available, but they also provide a smoothie with a delicious, ice cream–like consistency. You can also put fresh fruits in the freezer shortly before blending or freeze any leftover fruit to use the next time you make a smoothie.

THE CRUNCH FACTOR: Purists simply get a spoon and eat a smoothie bowl just as it is. But for a tasty and healthy treat, add additional toppings such as grains, nuts (hazelnuts, almonds), seeds (sunflower), or dried fruits. You can also try some of the trendy superfoods such as chia seeds, goji berries, or cacao nibs. If you can't decide, just use homemade granola (recipe follows), which always works and tastes great.

SUPERFOODS

ACAI POWDER: The acai berry is packed with antioxidants and is an unbeatable anti-aging weapon.

CHIA SEEDS: This special energy source is rich in omega-3-fatty acids and plenty of other valuable nutrients.

HEMP SEEDS/HEMP POWDER: Hemp is one of the best protein sources in the world. When used as a smoothie ingredient, it's best if the hemp seeds are peeled. Hemp powder is a good alternative.

GINGER: Ginger is known for its many positive effects on health. It energizes, strengthens the body's defenses, and warms the body and soul from the inside.

CACAO (RAW): Raw, natural cacao is rich in antioxidants. This energy booster is also a natural antidepressant and can help support weight loss.

CARDAMOM: One of the main spices used in Ayurvedic Medicine, cardamom helps digestion, reduces bloating, detoxifies the body from caffeine, and can improve lung function.

MACA POWDER: Used by the ancient Incan civilization, this legendary powder provides enhanced energy and increased stamina for starting and finishing every day.

SPIRULINA: This dark green algae is nearly pure chlorophyll and nicknamed the "Queen of Proteins." It is especially favored because of its detoxifying properties. You can also use chlorella powder.

STEVIA: This plant can replace sugar and honey as a sweetener. Due to its unique strong taste, you should use it only in small quantities.

STINGING NETTLES: If you have access to and are able to pick stinging nettles (make sure to use gloves or use a really tight grip), it is a great source of protein. The seeds are also very healthy.

GROUND ELDER: This wild spinach is full of vitamins and minerals.

KALE: Kale is among the healthiest of foods. Full of vitamins, minerals, and dietary fibers, it enriches any smoothie. Savoy cabbage makes a good kale replacement.

FLAXSEEDS: Flaxseeds are full of omega-3 fatty acids and dietary fibers and help with digestion.

DANDELION: Dandelion is a real miracle herb that stimulates the metabolism and is good for the liver.

BLOSSOMS: As a garnish, they're the icing on the cake. And it is really amazing how many blossoms are edible. The list includes daisies, violets, fuchsias, and rose petals. Just make sure to buy organic (no pesticide spray) or pick them in the wild (or from Grandma's yard when she is not looking...).

GOJI BERRIES: These are small miracle berries with a delicate, light, and sweet flavor. They're full of vitamin C and add a great color. Soak the berries for about half an hour before using.

COCONUT FLAKES AND COCONUT WATER: Coconut is a marvelous superfood with immune-boosting properties and provides much needed electrolytes.

9

SMOOTHIES
for you

Par & Sley 12
Mango to Tango 14
Jonny Kale 16
Goji-Queen/Aronia-Queen 18
Summer Dream 20
Halloween Smoothie 22
King Louie 24
Smoothie Mediterranean 26
Kale Rider 28
Gold Milk 30
Low Carb 32
Pink Power 34
Tropical Smoothie 36
Total Local Winter Smoothie .. 38
Mean Green Smoothie 40
Blueberry Dream 42
Hangover Cure 44
Chai Smoothie 46
Cacao Smoothie 48
Bloody Hell 50

PAR & SLEY

Here comes a great, healthy smoothie with apple, veggies, and the namesake parsley. The intense green color of the drink is invigorating and awakens the vital spirits.

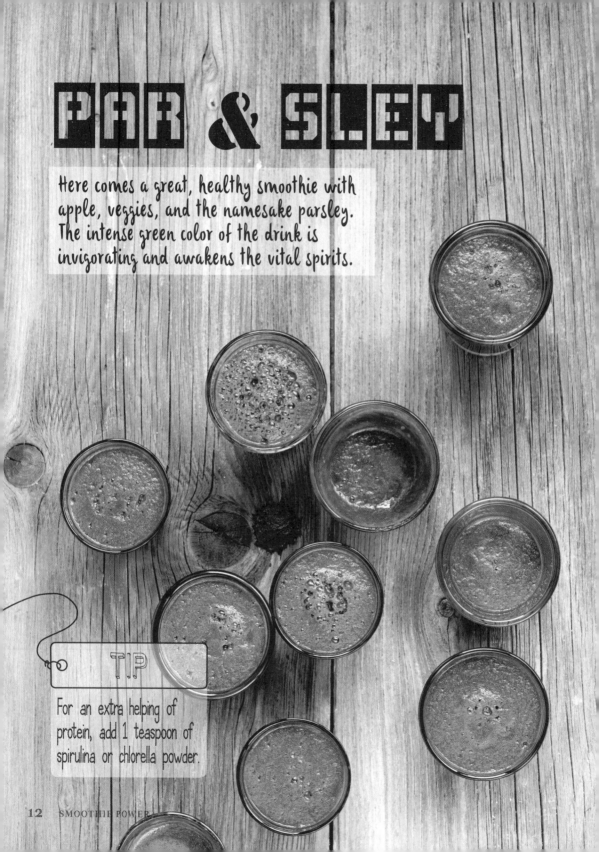

TIP

For an extra helping of protein, add 1 teaspoon of spirulina or chlorella powder.

SOME FRESH MINT

1 cup (60 g) fresh parsley

SWEETEN AS NEEDED WITH HONEY OR STEVIA

⅔ CUP (50 G) RAW BROCCOLI

1 STALK OF CELERY

⅔ cup (80 g) cucumber

ONE APPLE

1¼ CUP (300 ML) WATER

MANGO TO TANGO ♪

Mangoes are full of vitamins, are energizing, and are known in India as the "the fruit of the gods." In combination with fennel and orange, it makes for an unusual, revitalizing fruit experience.

½ CUP (100 ML)
WATER

½ CUP (100ML) ORANGE JUICE, *or* 1 ORGANIC ORANGE

PREFERABLY FRESHLY SQUEEZED

WITH SOME PEEL

1 medium ripe mango
(or dried, soaked
mango pieces [8–10])

About 1 cup
(80 g)
fresh fennel

TIP

Mango to Tango is a great
smoothie for kids. Because of the
sweetness, it is easy to sneak in
a lot of healthy vegetables.

JONNY KALE

This smoothie can be described as being refreshing, vibrantly green, and delicious. Using readily available oranges and bananas, it can be enjoyed in the summer as well as the winter, and it simply puts you in a good mood!

½ cup (120 ml) rice and coconut drink

1 banana

⅔ CUP (40 G) KALE

1 orange (whole slices without peel)

2

3

4 ICE CUBES

1

GOJI-QUEEN
ARONIA-QUEEN

The goji berry has been used in Traditional Tibetan Medicine and Traditional Chinese Medicine for more than 3,000 years. Now, the rest of the world is catching on to its status as a superfood. Another variation of the goji berry is the aronia berry, which gives the smoothie a yummy purple color instead of deep orange.

2 tbsp (11 g) goji berries

Always soak dried berries for a while and use the soaking liquid in the smoothie too.

or

2 tbsp (15 g) aronia berries

1 TBSP (20 G) MAPLE SYRUP OR HONEY

One banana

ONE APPLE

Some vanilla (powder or extract)

1¼ CUPS (300 ML) WATER

SUMMER DREAM

This is a refreshing summer drink for a hot day. It also makes a great party drink, with the addition of a shot of white rum. Done and done!

10 FRESH MINT
LEAVES OR
MORE

Juice of one lime

ICE CUBES
AS
NEEDED

About 5 cups (800 g)
watermelon

HALLOWEEN SMOOTHIE

HALLOWEEN SMOOTHIE

What do you get when you combine honey, pumpkin, orange, and banana? An unusual but unbelievably delicious smoothie! The nutty taste of the Hokkaido pumpkin and the fruity freshness of the orange harmonizes perfectly. The addition of cardamom gives it a little extra kick.

 **ADVICE**

For this recipe, you'll need to use a high performance blender because of pumpkin's consistency!

3/4 cup (200 ml) orange juice or 2 oranges peeled

+ WATER TO REACH THE DESIRED CONSISTENCY

1 tbsp (20 g) maple syrup or honey

1/4 tsp cardamom powder

1 banana

1 3/4 cups (200 G) HOKKAIDO PUMPKIN *raw with skin*

King Louie

Crispy because of the granola, chocolaty, and with banana and a hint of coconut flavor, this smoothie is a perfect substitute for breakfast. It is filling and offers everything you need for a great start to the day.

1 ripe banana

⅓ CUP (70 ML) MACADAMIA NUT MILK

2 tbsp (10 g) raw oats (not toasted)

1 tbsp (13 g) chia seeds

½ CUP (90 ML) COCONUT WATER

2 tbsp (8 g) unsweetened coconut flakes

Topping: 1 tsp cacao nibs

1 tsp raw and pure cacao powder

+ 4 ice cubes

SMOOTHIE MEDITERRANEAN

Are you longing for the blue Mediterranean Sea, summer, and the warming rays of the sun? This extravagant smoothie might just be the ticket. It's filled with vitamin C and the perfect combination of Mediterranean and Oriental flavors. You can almost hear the cicada buzzing . . . .

3-4 fresh figs

Juice of
half of a
lemon

3/4-1 1/4 cups
(200-300 ml)
water

1 pomegranate
(seeds only)

2-3
DATES

TIP

Remove the seeds from the
pomegranate in bowl filled with
water so it doesn't squirt!

KALE RIDER

Using kale in a smoothie? Yes! The pineapple and the coconut water make it sweet and delicious. The unusual combination will pleasantly surprise you!

2 TBSP (18 G)
AVOCADO

Juice of one lime

1 cup (150 g)
pineapple

1 handful (about 1 cup, or 60 g)
of kale (remove the stems) or
savoy cabbage

1 1/3 CUPS
(330 ML)
COCONUT WATER

TIP

Instead of coconut water,
you can also use regular
filtered water.

GOLD MILK

The star inside this smoothie is turmeric. It contains the substance curcumin, which has antioxidant and anti-inflammatory properties, making this miracle root a medicinal plant. On cold days, this sweet and simultaneously slightly spicy smoothie will warm your soul.

2-3 tbsp
(40-60 g)
maple syrup
or
4 dates

Small piece of
fresh ginger

ABOUT
1 THUMB LENGTH
(¾ OUNCE, OR
20 G) FRESH
TURMERIC ROOT
OR
1 TSP
TURMERIC POWDER

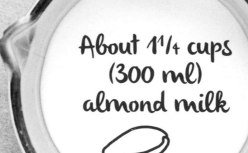

About 1¼ cups
(300 ml)
almond milk

LOW CARB

The mix of vegetables, fruits, and herbs, as well as a bit of spice from the ginger, makes this smoothie into something extra special. More importantly, it is full of valuable nutrients.

2½ TBSP (10 G) PARSLEY

¼ cup (60 ml) WATER

1 cup (30 g) spinach

1 medium

APPLE

1 handful (1/3 cup, or 60 g) of grapes

½ OF A YELLOW PEPPER

1 small piece of ginger

1 tbsp (15 ml) lemon juice

4 ice cubes

PINK POWER

How do you get your child to eat healthy red beets? Give them this Pink Power smoothie garnished with cacao nibs. It is sweet, refreshing, and oh so yummy!

Pretty ♡

Topping: a few cacao nibs

1/3 CUP (80 G) RED BEETS, RAW

1/2 cup (100 ml) water

3/4 cup (200 ml) almond or rice milk

3 tbsp (60 g) maple syrup or honey

SOME FRESH MINT

Tropical Smoothie

When locally available ingredients become scarce in the middle of winter and the days are just too dark, the tropical flavor of this smoothie will give you a pleasant escape. And with a little imagination, you may even be able to hear the sound of the ocean.

fresh cilantro, optional

One banana

1 PASSION FRUIT OR PAPAYA

Juice

lime

of one

½ CUP (100 ml) WATER

½ cup (30 g) coconut flakes (or ½ cup [100 ml] coconut water)

1¼ cups (200 G) PINEAPPLE

Total Local Winter Smoothie

This is a great smoothie for winter. The seasonal mix of red beets, kale, apple, and topinambour (Jerusalem artichoke) is colorful and delicious. It's guaranteed to make the season less gloomy. Topinambour, also called sunroot, is a rather unknown miracle root full of vitamins and iron.

TIP

Homegrown sprouts offer a great source of vitamins in the middle of winter.

Sweeten to taste

About ¼ cup (50 g) red beets, raw

ONE APPLE

About ⅓ cup (50 g) topinambur, raw

Tip

1 tsp hemp powder

1 handful of kale

¾ cup (200 ml) water

About half of a handful of blackberry leaves or fresh herbs

SPROUTS

1 tbsp (8 g) aronia berries (soaked)

MEAN GREEN SMOOTHIE

Here comes an absolutely powerful and medicinal drink. The greens are randomly exchangeable, but the darker the greens, the better. During the summer, if possible, use wild herbs such as dandelion, stinging nettles, ash weed, and clover. In the winter, you can use readily available kale.

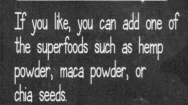

TIP

If you like, you can add one of the superfoods such as hemp powder, maca powder, or chia seeds.

One handful of greens, i.e.:

1 apple

KALE

GINGER,
SLICED

Mache lettuce
(lamb's lettuce)

unpeeled

1 piece of
cucumber

HERBS

OINE BIAINIAINA

1 tbsp (12 g) flax seeds,
milled

ABOUT 1¼ CUP (300 ML) WATER

BLUEBERRY DREAM

Sweet and still healthy, this smoothie is a blueberry lover's dream. Even kids like this "blueberry milk." If you add less water, you will get a thicker consistency that makes for a healthy and delicious jam.

Shredded coconut for garnish

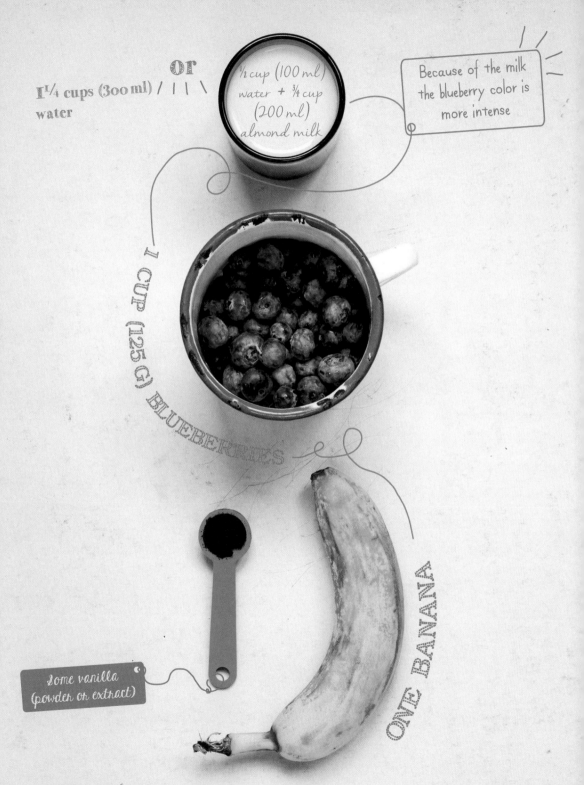

1¼ cups (300 ml) water

or

½ cup (100 ml) water + ¾ cup (200 ml) almond milk

Because of the milk the blueberry color is more intense

1 CUP (125 G) BLUEBERRIES

Some vanilla (powder or extract)

ONE BANANA

Hangover Cure

This exotic, green smoothie with mango, avocado, banana, and grapes awakens and revitalizes the body. The chia seeds make it a really powerful drink.

For topping: ½ tsp chia seeds

½ of a mango

½ cup (40 g) kale

2 tbsp (20 g) avocado

½ of a banana

1 HANDFUL (⅓ cup, 60 G) OF GRAPES

½ cup (100 ml) coconut water

1 TBSP (13 G) CHIA SEEDS

¼ cup (50 ml) rice milk

4 ICE CUBES

CHAI SMOOTHIE

Enjoy this smoothie served over ice on hot days. On cold days, it tastes best warmed up. Like Indian Chia tea, this smoothie delivers with its sweet, aromatic, slightly spicy, and cinnamon-y taste.

3 TBSP (60 G) MAPLE SYRUP OR HONEY

¼ tsp nutmeg
(freshly grated is best)

¼ tsp cardamom powder

½–1 TSP CINNAMON

1 piece of fresh ginger

1¹/4 cups
(300 ml)
almond milk

SOME VANILLA
POWDER OR EXTRACT

CACAO SMOOTHIE

Anybody who was Nutella crazy as a child will love this smoothie version. In a nutshell, this smoothie is simply genius. It is a tasty and very healthy alternative for a hot or cold cocoa drink. The salt brings out the sweetness even more.

3 TBSP (60 G)
MAPLE SYRUP OR
HONEY

ABOUT ½ CUP (60 G)
SOAKED (POSSIBLY
ROASTED) HAZELNUTS
OR BRAZIL NUTS

½ cup (100 ml)
WATER

1 tbsp (5 g)
raw
cacao powder

3/4 cup
(200 ml)
almond milk

TIP

If you are a fan of thin
chocolate mints, add fresh or
dry mint.

some vanilla
(powder or extract)

1 pinch of salt

BLOODY HELL

A very nifty and well thought out mix of grapes, red beets, orange juice, and mint delivers an intense, beautiful purple color and a taste that leaves you wanting more.

4 MINT LEAVES

4 ice cubes

1 RED BEET

1 Tbsp (12 g) Flax SEEDs

Red and green grapes
1 handful ⅓ cup (60 g)
of each

1 tsp lemon juice

1 tsp acai powder

½ CUP (100 ML) FRESHLY
SQUEEZED ORANGE JUICE

Green SMOOTHIES

Bloody & Berry 54
Rock It Baby 56
A-Game 58
Always full 60
Sexy Thing 62
Mexican Mango 64
Road Drink 66
Garden Dream 68
Wild Child   70
Pineapple Express 72
Green Lemonade 74
Honey & Tini 76
Iron King 78
Green Machine 80
Power Bomb 82
Happy Pear 84
Magic Manni 86
Arugula Rocket 88
Goa Beach 90
Bro-Juice 92

BLOODY & BERRY

The combination of strawberries and basil is a classic summer mix for gourmets around the world. Strawberries are packed with vitamin C, have very few calories, and simply taste great. Basil, also known as "the king of herbs," offers valuable nutrients, which will make you feel perhaps a little more royal.

1 1/2 cups (250 g) strawberries

1/2 CUP (100 ML) WATER

1/2 of a banana

About 1/3 cup (8–10 g) basil leaves

OPTIONAL: 2–3 CARDAMOM PODS

ROCK IT BABY

Arugula rocks. For this smoothie, the spicy taste of arugula, also called rucola, and the fruity fresh orange unite. It's superb! The peel of the orange is considered a valuable source of nutrition, so throw that in too. Just make sure to use only organic produce that has not been sprayed with pesticide.

½ CUP (100 ML) WATER

1 organic orange

with some peel

1½ cups (30 g) ARUGULA

½ of a banana

OPTIONAL:

SWEETEN TO TASTE WITH COCONUT SUGAR

A-GAME

Apples, dates, spinach, avocado, and grapes—this is a powerful and healthy drink to help you stay fit. It is great to take on-the-go or to bring to the gym.

1½ cups (50 g) spinach

1 cup (110 g) ...

apple

2-3 dates

1 tsp chia seeds

⅓ CUP (40 G) GRAPES

1 TBSP {8 G} AVOCADO

⅔ CUP (160 G) RICE AND COCONUT DRINK

Ice cubes as needed

Always Full

Without a doubt, kale is the new superfood. With so many vitamins, minerals, and dietary fibers, this vegetable has a nourishing impact on the body. Mixed with avocado, which contains plenty of healthy fats, it adds up to a delicious and super healthy green smoothie.

tip

If you want to include the nutritious kiwi peel, make sure to use organic produce.

munch

1 handful (about ½ cup, or 30–40 g) of savoy cabbage without stalk or kale

¾ CUP (200 ML) WATER

1 KIWI

1 TSP COCONUT SUGAR OR XYLITOL

1 pear

¼ OF AN AVOCADO

Sexy Thing
Sexy Thing

This is almost like a real beach cocktail-only better. It's packed with valuable minerals, antioxidants, and chlorophyll. The tropical flavor creates a happy mood, and it tastes like a glorious day full of sun, beach, and ocean.

¾ CUP (200 ML) WATER

About ⅔ cup (10 g)
cilantro

1½ cups (250 g)

1 tbsp (9 g)
avocado

p i n e a p p l e

⅓ cup (20 g)
coconut flakes

1 tbsp (8 g) sesame seeds
also great roasted but they have
fewer nutrients

MEXICAN MANGO

Spinach, fruits, and almond milk make for a very healthy and super delicious smoothie. Because the ingredients are pulverized in a high performance blender, the nutrients can be readily absorbed by the body.

1⅓ cups (40 g) spinach

⅔ cup (170 g) almond milk

1¼ cups (200 g) mango

½ CUP (70 G) GREEN GRAPES

2 TSP AGAVE NECTAR

Ice cubes

ROAD DRINK

Stinging nettles are so healthy. Together with apricots and peaches, it makes a refreshing and sweet summer cocktail. Spirulina powder adds an extra punch of protein and gives this smoothie a deep green color.

GO

1 HANDFUL
(ABOUT ¼–⅓ CUP,
OR 20–30 G)
OF STINGING NETTLE LEAVES
(WITH SEEDS TOO)

¾ CUP (200 ML)
WATER

1 TBSP
(9 G)
AVOCADO

4 5
3 6
2 7
1 8

Fresh
(or
dried)
apricots

3 PEACHES

1 tsp spirulina

Garden Dream

This is a smoothie made from locally grown superfoods. Dandelion greens offer an abundance of healthy nutrients, raspberries and dates add the necessary sweetness, and mint gives this power drink its fresh kick.

tip

If picking your own, pick only small to medium sized dandelion greens. Because they are younger, the smaller leaves are tender and more nutritious.

²/₃ CUP (150 ML) WATER

1½ CUPS (200 G) RASPBERRIES

DATES

4 - 5

About 12 mint leaves

Half of a handful (about ½ cup, or 20 g) of dandelion greens

Wild Child

Ground elder is a lot more than an annoying weed. This valuable healing plant is rich in vitamins and minerals, as well as readily available during the summer. The addition of sweet fruits turns this smoothie into a real power drink.

²/₃ CUP (150 ML) WATER

2 tbsp (26 g) chia seeds

About ²/₃ cup (20 g) ground elder

1 banana

1½ cups (250 g) apricots

(WITHOUT PITS)

Topping:
some more hemp powder

Pineapple Express

Muesli plus smoothie, this makes a delicious and filling breakfast. The pineapple wakes up your spirits in the morning, and the banana offers essential calcium for a great way to start the day.

¾ cup (130 g) pineapple

⅔ cup (100 g) frozen banana

2–3 dates

¼ cup (15 g) muesli

⅓ CUP (80 ML) OAT MILK

1 ⅓ cups (40 g) spinach

1 tbsp (5 g) hemp protein powder

4 ice cubes

Green Lemonade

You can make lemonade? Yes, but only if it is healthy. This sparkling smoothie has a vibrant taste reminiscent of summer: fresh and green like the meadow, sparkling like a summer rain, and just plain yummy. Mint, with its many healing properties, adds a pleasant kick.

½ CUP (100 ML) WATER

Optional:
½ cup (100 ml) sparkling water

About 12 mint leaves

Juice of one organic
LIME or LEMON

[WITH SOME PEEL]

2 TSP (6 G)
COCONUT SUGAR
OR (8 G) XYLITOL

Half of a large cucumber
(ABOUT 2 CUPS, OR 300G)

HONEY & TINI ♡

Mmmm . . . that tastes just like summertime. Honeydew melon is rich in vitamins, sugary sweet, and lends the smoothie its beautiful color. On hot days, just simply add ice cubes for a delicious and healthy summer drink.

Topping: some lemon zest

2 CUPS (350G) HONEYDEW MELON

Mint leaves to taste

JUICE OF ONE *organic* LEMON

3-4 ICE CUBES

Iron King

We're adding parsley to a smoothie? Yes, because this herb is more than just a decoration for the plate. It is packed with essential iron. Together with the fennel and oranges, it makes a delightful healthy cocktail at its finest.

½ OF A HANDFUL OF PARSLEY

2/3 CUP (150 ML) WATER

2 ORGANIC ORANGES (with some peel)

1 cup (80 g) fennel

green
MACHINE

Go green power! This iron-containing
cocktail tastes great and is also very
nutritious. Pascal celery is a real
nutrient-packed addition, and
the ginger adds a little
extra zing.

2/3 CUP (140 ML)
WATER

1/4 CUP (15 G)
PARSLEY

1/2 tsp
olive oil

I slice of
GINGER

1/3 CUP (40 G) PASCAL CELERY
with leaves

2 tsp (10 g)
agave nectar

2/3 CUP (80 G)
CUCUMBER
WITHOUT SEEDS

1 slice of lemon

4 ice cubes

1 cup (150 G) MANGO

POWER BOMB

Kale and mango? A healthier superfood combination is hardly possible. This fruity fresh mixture keeps you fit and gives you enough energy for the whole day. Smoothies made with kale are rapidly becoming all the trend.

One **mango**

⅔–¾ CUP
(150–200 ML)
WATER

1 TBSP (15 G) FLAX SEEDS

1 HANDFUL OF *kale*

The flax seeds are split up nicely in a high-performance blender and help digestion.

HAPPY PEAR

"And here comes the colorful fall." The good old pear contains antioxidants, dietary fiber, B vitamins, and boosts the immune system. With the addition of peeled hemp seeds, all mixed to creamy perfection, this smoothie offers delicious and nutritious support for the arrival of the first cold days. As a side note, the title is homage to the best café in Ireland.

4-6 DATES

3 TBSP (23 G) PEELED HEMP SEEDS

2 pears

½ of a handful of parsley

½ CUP (100 ML) WATER

MAGIC MANNI

Chard is a super source of chlorophyll and iron.
Grapes offer fast energy, but make sure to use only
organic and pesticide-free. Together with chia seeds,
this drink quickly conquers any tiredness.

²/₃ CUP (150 ML) WATER

1 handful (about 2 cups, or 80 g) of chard (without stalk)

8–10 green grapes

2 tbsp (26 g) CHIA SEEDS

1 banana

ARUGULA ROCKET

Chlorophyll, fruit, and nuts makes for a wonderful combination. Arugula is very healthy, offering an abundance of iron and calcium. And instead of purchasing arugula at the market, you can pick wild arugula, if you can find it.

2/3 cup (150 g)
walnut milk

1 1/3 cups (150 g)
apple

1/2 cup (85 g) banana

1 1/2 cups
(30 g)
arugula

4 ICE CUBES

Goa Beach

Here's another beach cocktail: exotic, tropical, and sensual. Papaya, called "the fruit of the angels" by Christopher Columbus, is super healthy. Red chile peppers stimulate the metabolism and warms you up from the inside.

Toppings: a few coconut flakes or a handful of papaya seeds

½ CUP (100 ML) WATER

alternative: coconut water

Juice of an organic lime

with some PEEL

½ of a papaya (about 3½–4 cups, or 500–600 g)

with seeds

A FEW MINT LEAVES to taste

1 small piece of chile pepper (red)

2 tbsp (8 g) coconut flakes

BRO-*Juice*

Broccoli is detoxifying and one of the healthiest vegetables there is. Combined with the warming and spicy ginger, it makes a tasty winter smoothie that packs a punch.

Juice of one
LEMON

2 organic
ORANGES [WITH SOME PEEL]

1 TBSP (9 G)
avocado

1 small piece of
GINGER

1 CUP (70 G)
broccoli
[TOPS WITHOUT STALK]

SMOOTHIES
for kids

Mr. Strawberry 96
Banana Joe 98
Pink Milk 100
Johnny Blue 102
Dragon Juice 104
MacCucumber 106
Princess Melonie 108
South Pacific Dream 110
Raspberry Dragon 112
Flu Shake 114
Banana Coco Joe 116
Green Mouse 118
Big Fig 120
Chocorangina 122
Green Limo 124
DaNuMi 126
Brocco Lilly 128
KaCo 130
Mango Mandy 132
Fit Kid 134

Mr. Strawberry

Behold the awesome, bright red, juicy strawberry. They're great for the immune system, so tasty, and so versatile. For instance, here they are blended into a summer smoothie with mint. Mint leaves are not just for garnish. They contain potent antioxidants and are a known remedy to aid digestion.

Optional: Cacao nibs, for decoration

½ CUP
(100 ML) WATER

About 12 mint leaves

HALF OF A BANANA

1½ cups (250 g) strawberries

BANANA JOE

The stinging nettle is a real miracle herb. It is chock full of iron and seems like it grows everywhere. Once you make friends with it, it will be a friend for life. To mask its bitter taste, combine with plenty of fruit.

1 KID'S HANDFUL (ABOUT ¼ CUP, OR 20 G) OF STINGING NETTLES, WITH SEEDS BUT WITHOUT STEMS

²/₃ CUP (150 ML) WATER

ONE KIWI

I APPLE

ONE BANANA

Pink Milk

This is an unusual smoothie-extremely delicious, rich and creamy, and also very pink. The rose is used in Ayurvedic Medicine and is known for its soothing, calming, and anti-inflammatory effects. And the red beets are full of nitrates and antioxidants. This smoothie will really boost your mood.

1 RED ORGANIC ROSE BLOSSOM

ONE QUARTER OF A RED BEET

Coconut sugar or (12 G) xylitol (9 G)

1 TBSP (9 G)

1-1¼ CUPS (250-300 G) ALMOND OR OAT MILK

2 TBSP (15 G) PEELED HEMP SEEDS

Johnny Blue

Here's another fantastic summertime smoothie. Blueberries and sweet banana provide plenty of vitamin C and potassium for the body. The color purple will remind you of those warm summer nights, making you long for more.

¾ CUP (200 ML)
WATER

① banana

1–1½ cups
(150–200 g)
blueberries

½ of a kid's handful
(about ½ cup, or 25 g)
of dandelion greens

OPTIONAL:

SWEETEN TO TASTE WITH
COCONUT SUGAR

DRAGON JUICE

Sound the ground elder alarm! Ground elder, also called bishop's weed due to its shape, tastes a little like celery and is rich in vitamin C and antioxidants. The minced leaves can also be made into a poultice to be used on burns and insect bites for quick relief.

2/3 CUP (150 ML) WATER

5-6 dates
to taste

1 TBSP (12 G) FLAX SEEDS

½ OF A KID'S HANDFUL (ABOUT 1 CUP, OR 25 G) OF GROUND ELDER

2 bananas

MacCucumber

Cucumbers are great for aiding digestion, rehydrating the body, and replenishing vitamins. Combined with mint, they simply taste refreshing. Served over ice cubes, MacCucumber is the perfect drink for a hot summer day.

Tip
This smoothie is also yummy if you use coconut water instead.

2/3 CUP (150 ML) WATER

1 apple

1 TBSP (9 G) COCONUT SUGAR
OR (12 G) XYLITOL

½ of a cucumber.

About 12 mint leaves

Juice of half of a lemon

Princess Melonie

This smoothie has plenty of vitamin A, tastes like sunshine in a glass, and thanks to the addition of the chia seeds, is a superfood party. A small piece of organic lemon peel only adds to the refreshment.

3—4 ICE CUBES

Optional:
mint leaves

1 tbsp (15 g) chia seeds

Juice of one lemon

¼ of a watermelon (about 3 cups, or 500 g)

South Pacific Dream

Mmmm . . . mango. Since ancient times, mango has been called "the fruit of the gods" in India because of its sweetness and gold yellow color. A ripe mango smells sweet and the flesh gives way lightly to pressure. Combined with banana and lime, this smoothie transports you to a beach in the tropics.

Tip

If desired, you can replace the lime with a lemon.

3/4 CUP (200 ML) WATER

1 Kid's handful (about ⅔ cup, or 20 g) of spinach

One mango (about 1¾ cups, or 300 g)

Juice of one lime

2 tbsp (15 g) coconut flakes

ONE BANANA

RASPBERRY DRAGON

Raspberries not only taste heavenly, but they're full of vitamins, minerals, and antioxidants. Goji berries add a brilliant color, and the chia seeds are what give this smoothie its "dragon powers."

OPTIONAL:

1 TBSP (9 G) COCONUT SUGAR
OR (12 G) XYLITOL

1¼ cups (150g)
raspberries

1 tbsp (6 g)
goji berries
soaked

1 tbsp (13 g)
chia seeds

¼ cup (50 g) red beets

½ CUP (100 ML)
WATER

FLU SHAKE

Here is an anti-flu drink at its finest, packed with vitamin C. The ginger strengthens the immune system and warms from within. Be generous with the honey; the sweetness will boost your spirits and make you happy again.

Tip

Ginger can be very spicy. When you first start, use a small amount and gradually increase to suit your taste.

2/3 CUP (150 ML) WATER

Juice of ½ of an organic orange **WITH PEEL**

JUICE OF ONE LEMON

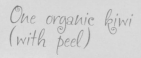

A COUPLE OF SLICES OF GINGER (TO TASTE)

One organic kiwi (with peel)

1 APPLE

1 TSP HONEY

BANANA COCO

This tropical drink will remind you of an exciting adventure on a South Pacific island. Delicious hemp seeds create a nice creamy texture and are also great sprinkled on top. As an alternative, you can use coconut flakes as a garnish instead.

JOE

1 TBSP (8 G) COCONUT FLAKES

1 tsp peeled hemp seeds

one ♥ banana

3/4 cup (200 ml) rice and coconut drink

About 4-5 dates

Green Mouse

This is the fusion of sweet and green. The pineapple makes you wish you were on vacation, and the spinach tastes much better in a smoothie than when its cooked—I promise.

1 KID'S HANDFUL (ABOUT 1 CUP, OR 30 G) OF SPINACH

1 organic kiwi (with peel)

1⅓ cups (200 g) pineapple

1 tbsp (8 g) peeled hemp seeds

¾ CUP (200 ML) WATER

Big Fig

This is a fig dream from *A Thousand and One Nights*. This smoothie is filling and a great replacement for breakfast. Once the drink is topped off with cinnamon, the sweet and warm taste will whisk you off to a spice market in the Orient.

Tip
Dried figs can be used instead of fresh figs.

4

FIGS,

soaked

1

banana

1 PINCH OF CINNAMON

1 CUP
(250 ML)
ALMOND MILK

ONE KID'S HANDFUL
(about ¼ cup, or 40 g)
of almonds, soaked

Tip

Add 2 tsp (8 g) of flax seeds to make the smoothie even more nutritious.

Chocorangina

This is a special smoothie for magical moments because the combination of cacao and oranges evokes memories of the holiday season. Hemp seeds are not only healthy, but also are quite filling. The hemp seeds should be coarsely ground before being added to the blender.

1 tbsp (5 g) raw cacao powder

1 tbsp (8 g) peeled hemp seeds

1–2 tbsp (9–18 g) coconut sugar or (12–24 g) xylitol

3/4 CUP (200 ML) ALMOND OR OAT MILK

Juice of one orange

OPTIONAL:

A FEW CACAO NIBS, ADDED FOR GARNISH TOO

Green Limo

This is a really simple lemonade drink, but much healthier than traditional lemonade. It combines banana for the sweetness, spinach for the chlorophyll, lemon for the fizz, and dates for that little something extra.

Tip

The spinach can be replaced by mache lettuce, also known as lamb's lettuce.

3/4 CUP (200 ML) WATER

Juice of one lemon

2-3 ice cubes
[IN THE SUMMER]

1-2 KID'S HANDFUL (ABOUT 1 CUP, OR 30 G) OF SPINACH

5-6 DATES

1 ba na na

DaNuMi

Da=Dates, Nu=Nut, Mi=Milk

This is a really simple nut shake, which is great for breakfast or break time. If you add the hemp seeds, it becomes even more nutritious. If you prefer a lighter smoothie, you can replace a portion of the nut milk with regular filtered water.

Tip

If you're using a high-performance blender, you can use Brazil nuts instead.

mmh

5-7 dates

1 CUP (100 G) WALNUTS OR
(135 G) HAZELNUTS,
SOAKED AND DRAINED

1 PINCH OF CINNAMON

1 cup (250 ml) oat milk

OPTIONAL:
peeled hemp seeds to
add a boost of nutrition

BroccoLilly

Broccoli is a total nutrient powerhouse. It is great for the muscles, the immune system, and protects against illness in general. Chia seeds give the smoothie its potency, and if you prefer your drink a little more sweet, you can add more banana.

1 cup (80g) broccoli tops

1 banana

one apple

1 TSP CHIA SEEDS

1 TSP coconut sugar or xylitol

KaCo

Ka=Kale Co=Coconut
This is an established,
healthy, powerful drink.
And trust me, this is the
way kale tastes best. But
you have to try it before
you can believe it. So
ready, set, and go!

Tip

You can replace the
coconut water with regular
filtered water.

2-3 kale leaves (or savoy cabbage), without stalk

One pear

1 cup (250 g) coconut water

one banana

5-6 dates

MANGO MANDY

This drink is dedicated to a friend named Mandy. Tangerines are packed into this smoothie. It has a glowing color and is so detectibly sweet, like an orange dream.

3 TANGERINES

1/2–2/3 CUP (100–150 ML) WATER

1 TBSP (6 G)

GOJI BERRIES, SOAKED

1 mango

Fit Kid

Combining celery with orange? What, you've never heard of it? That's crazy. With this smoothie, you'll never be unwell again. If you prefer a stronger orange flavor, you can substitute more orange juice for the water. The parsley adds an extra helping of iron.

Tip

Add 1 tbsp (13 g) soaked chia seeds to this smoothie to get even more superpower!

2 stalks of celery

2/3 CUP (150 ML) WATER

Some parsley

Juice of 2-3 oranges

1 apple

Sweeten to taste

SMOOTHIE

Bowls

White Star 138
Peaches of Cream 140
Pink Elephant 142
Indian Summer 144
Hello, Charlie Brown! 146
Peppy Paprika 148
Green Oasis 150
Pea for Tea 152
Mellow Yellow 154
Pink Salad 156
Island in the Sun 158
Pinky Pie 160
Choco Shock 162
Blue Velvet 164
Cherry Kiss 166
Mister Muesli 168
Green Princess 170
Evergreen 172
Bombay Bowl 174
Golden Fall 176

White Star ☆

This smoothie bowl is a vision of white and guaranteed to be better than any chocolate coconut bar. Using cacao nibs as a topping not only adds a super-power-food but also adds a super-crunch-factor.

Toppings

1 baby pineapple

2 tbsp (15 g) coconut flakes

3 dried dates

1 tbsp (9 g) cacao nibs

CORE OF
½ OF A VANILLA BEAN

¾ CUP (200 ML)
RICE AND COCONUT
DRINK

1 big banana

2 tbsp (10 g)
shredded coconut

2 tbsp 10 g oats

1 TBSP (13 G) CHIA SEEDS

TO TASTE:
1–2 TSP (7–13 G)
AGAVE NECTAR

Peaches & Cream

Sun-ripened yellow peaches combined with creamy almond cream gives this smoothie its genuine Southern charm. During the summer months, this bowl is pleasantly filling but still heavenly light.

Toppings

2 tbsp (12 g) almonds

½ of a mango, cubed

1 handful of blackberries

To taste:
1 tbsp (20 g) honey
or maple syrup

1 tbsp (8 g) pistachios

1 TSP HONEY

3 TBSP (15 G)
FIVE GRAIN FLAKES

2 TBSP (32 G) ALMOND CREAM

½ OF A MANGO

2**
peaches
or nectarines
***

JUICE OF ½
OF AN ORANGE

Pink ELEPHANT

Packed with fresh berries, banana, and coconut yogurt, this smoothie bowl is simply gigantic. Topped with even more fresh berries, our Always-Works-Super-Crunchy-Granola, and fresh mint, this smoothie bowl should be a hit with people of all ages.

Toppings

3 tbsp (23 g) Always-Works-Super-Crunchy-Granola (see recipe on page 7)

Fresh mint

Mixed berries, i. e. strawberries, raspberries, blackberries, or blueberries

1 tbsp (20 g) honey

3 TBSP (45 G) COCONUT YOGURT

1 small banana

¾ CUP (100 G) RASPBERRIES

¾ CUP (100 G) STRAWBERRIES

INDIAN SUMMER

Taking advantage of that late summer harvest, the best summer and fall fruits are combined with crunchy nuts and red beets in a blender. This smoothie bowl strengthens the body's immune system and is guaranteed to prevent runny noses.

Toppings

1 tbsp (8 g) dried cranberries

1 tbsp (7 g) hazelnut slices

1 tbsp (15 g) blossom pollen

2 tbsp (22 g) popped quinoa or (26 g) amaranth

To taste: 1 tbsp (20 g) maple syrup

½ CUP (100 ML) HAZELNUT MILK

1 small
red beet

2 TBSP (15 G) DRIED CRANBERRIES

¼ tsp cinnamon

12 hazelnuts

10 red
(or purple) grapes

1 apple

2 plums

HELLO, CHARLIE BROWN!

Everyone who thinks that the peanut is simply a fattening snack food is just plain wrong. Just like other nuts, peanuts provide plenty of proteins and healthy fats. That's why I say: "Welcome to the bowl, Charlie Brown!"

Toppings

1 each yellow and green kiwi, sliced

2 tbsp (19 g) red currant

1 tbsp (8 g) sesame seeds

⅓ OF A PAPAYA

¼ tsp ground
cardamom

1 tbsp (16 g) peanut butter

1 small yellow
(or red) Beet

Juice of one
lime

1

mango

HALF OF A BANANA

BIG

SMALL

Peppy Paprika

Here, paprika and red chile flakes add that special kick for a powerful start to your day. With the right amount and in combination with the fruit and coconut, it is pleasantly peppy but not too spicy.

Toppings

1 banana, sliced

Sprinkle on top of banana:

1 tbsp (13 g) chia seeds

1 tbsp (9 g) coconut sugar

1 tbsp (5 g) shredded coconut

⅛–¼ tsp paprika or red chile flakes

1 PERSIMMON

½ OF AN ORANGE PEPPER

½ OF A SMALL MANGO

2–3 DASHES OF LEMON JUICE

To taste:
1 TBSP (20 G) AGAVE NECTAR

10 groundcherries

Green Oasis

What do thirsty desert hikers dream of? Of lush greens, sweet dates, coconut palms, and juicy pomegranates. This smoothie bowl is extremely refreshing and gives you energy and strength to finish your nature hike—or just to finish the day.

Toppings

2 tbsp (10 g) shredded coconut

10 pecans, coarsely chopped

3–4 tbsp (about 40 g) pomegranate seeds

⅔ CUP (50 G) YOUNG
KALE LEAVES

¾ cup (180 g)
coconut milk

1½ cups
(250 g)

pineapple,

peeled

3 dried
(MEDJOOL) DATES

1/2
OF AN
AVOCADO

PEA FOR TEA

Do you also like those paper-thin chocolate mints?
Then you'll love this power bowl with its protein-rich
peas, refreshing mint, and crunchy cacao nibs topping.

Toppings

½ of a green apple,
cut into a fan

1 tbsp (9 g) cacao nibs

1 tbsp (13 g) popped amaranth

1 YELLOW *or* GREEN KIWI

8 MINT LEAVES

½ CUP (70 G) FROZEN PEAS

1 BIG BANANA

Mellow Yellow

A piece of healthy, green celery and an abundance of yellow fruits is combined with something crispy, something crunchy, and a pinch of something salty on top. That's how a tame fruit salad is turned into a soothing cool breakfast.

Toppings

1 tbsp (11 g) banana chips, broken apart

1 tbsp (8 g) dried cranberries

2 tbsp (18 g) roasted salted peanuts

1 stalk of celery

½ OF A BANANA

Half of a mango

Yellow KIWI

Juice of ½ of an orange

⅔ cup (100 g) pineapple

Pink Salad

Here's a salad that's meant to be eaten with a spoon. Bright pink in color and wonderful in flavor, it's better than raspberry ice cream for breakfast. The combination of tasty mixed berries and robust superfoods unite and add pep to your day. Who can resist that?

Toppings

3–4 strawberries

2 tbsp (26 g) chia seeds

2 tbsp (18 g) sunflower seeds

2 tbsp (18 g) blueberries

1 TBSP (15 ML) LIME JUICE

1 AVOCADO

½ cup (100 g) frozen raspberries

6 green grapes

5

4

3

2

1

3 leaves of roman lettuce

ISLAND IN THE SUN

Mango, banana, and lime . . . the only thing missing from this tropical paradise now is the coconut. Well, coconut yogurt is dolloped on top to form a luscious floating island amidst a sea of deliciousness. Enjoy your vacation!

Toppings

Fresh mint

1 passion fruit

3 tbsp (45 g) coconut yogurt

Juice

OF
HALF OF
A LIME

1
2
3
4
5
6

strawberries

2 stalks of
LEMON
GRASS

1
banana

½ OF A
MANGO

Pinky Pie

This is for all little (and big!) girls who love colorful little ponies and dainty sweet cakes. This smoothie bowl tastes like berry cheesecake, but contains only healthy and wholesome ingredients, with a little drizzle of sweetness to top it all off.

Toppings

1 tbsp (8 g) chopped pistachios

1 tbsp (7 g) almond slivers

10 small strawberries

2 tbsp (40 g) honey or maple syrup

1 handful of raspberries

10 frozen strawberries

⅓ cup (80 g) frozen raspberries

1 TBSP (15 ML) LIME JUICE

1 whole grain melba toast

CORE OF HALF OF A VANILLA BEAN

1 small avocado

2/3 cup (150 ml) almond milk

Choco Shock

Here's a recipe for Pear Belle Helene rebooted and updated. This is how to create an incredibly delicious and trendy breakfast taking inspiration from a dated old-school dessert. PS: Some people also enjoy this as a dessert instead.

Toppings

½ of a pear, cut into small cubes

2 tbsp (15 g) dried cranberries

2 tbsp (18 g) cacao nibs

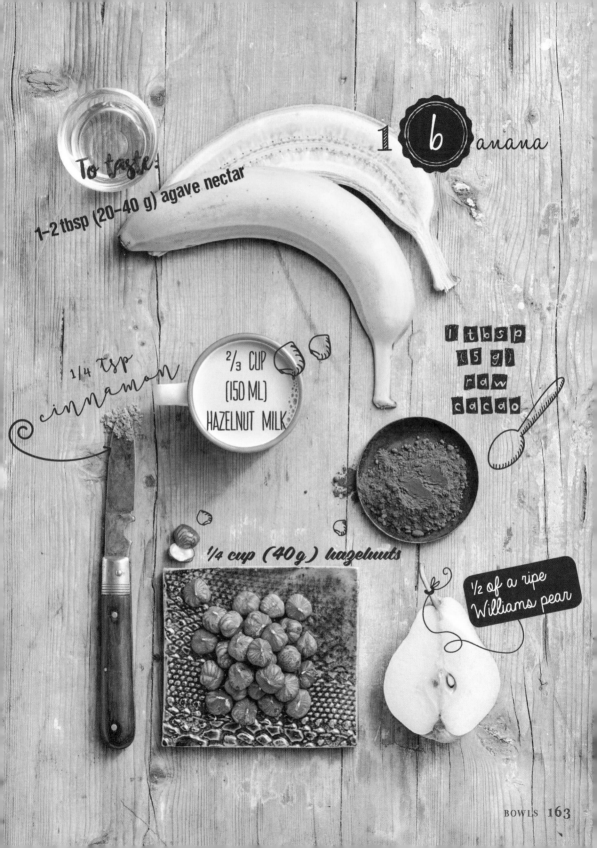

To taste:
1–2 tbsp (20–40 g) agave nectar

1 **b** anana

1/4 tsp cinnamon

²⁄₃ CUP (150 ML) HAZELNUT MILK

1 tbsp (5 g) raw cacao

1/4 cup (40 g) hazelnuts

1/2 of a ripe Williams pear

Blue Velvet

Here's an effective beauty cream that works from the inside. This smoothie bowl not only contains the tropical acai berry, but also raspberries, blueberries, blackberries, and even mulberries. All these berries are packed with nutrients and antioxidants, which will help keep your skin soft and smooth.

Toppings

2 tbsp (18 g) blueberries

2 tbsp (22 g) pomegranate seeds

2 tbsp (15 g) dried mulberries

1 3/4 oz (50 g) frozen

ACAI PUREE

½ of a
vanilla bean

JUICE OF
HALF OF AN ORANGE

¼ CUP (40 G) FROZEN
SOUR CHERRIES,
pitted

To taste:
1 Tbsp (20 g) agave nectar

¼ CUP (40 G)
EACH
raspberries,

BLUEBERRIES,

blackberries

1 small
BANANA

Cherry Kiss

In this smoothie bowl, cherries meet bananas and smooth almond cream and combine together in perfect creamy harmony. What a wonderful way to be kissed awake every morning.

Toppings

1 tbsp (9 g) cacao nibs

1 tbsp (7 g) almond slivers

2 tbsp (26 g) amaranth or (22 g) quinoa, popped

1 cup (150 g) frozen sour cherries (pitted)

2/3 cup (150 ml) almond milk

1 TBSP (16 G) ALMOND CREAM

Core of ½ of a vanilla bean

2 small bananas

Mister Muesli

Mixing granola with vegetables? Yes, and what a vegetable it is. The powerful parsnip root provides not only a lot of vitamin C, but it also keeps you full and satisfied for a long time.

Toppings

1 tbsp (12 g) flax seeds

1 tbsp (9 g) raisins

1 handful of blueberries

2 tbsp (14 g) hazelnut slices

3 TBSP (15 G)
FIVE GRAIN
FLAKES

¼ tsp

cinnamon

¾ cup (180 ml)
almond milk

2 TBSP
(28 ML)
LEMON JUICE

½ cup (50 g)
parsnip

1 APPLE

BANANA

Green Princess

Your vitamin C-rich greenness cordially invites you to spoon
and eat one's fill. fresh herbs, lemony fizz, and flavorful
fruit is the perfect adornment for any breakfast table.

Toppings

1 tbsp (13 g) chia seeds

1 tbsp (8 g) sesame seeds

1 tbsp (6 g) goji berries

1 apple

2 handfuls of spinach

1 TBSP (15 ML) LEMON JUICE

1 banana

6 branches of basil

1 KIWI

EVERGREEN

This smoothie bowl really has everything it needs to be a zesty and savory dish that's just perfect for lunch. Skip the usual cheese toast and cold cut sandwiches and try something green instead. You have to admit—it's delicious, right?

Toppings

2 tbsp (4 g) radish sprouts

5 cherry tomatoes

To taste: Shichimi Togarashi, or Japanese Seven Spice, to sprinkle on top

2 tbsp (28 ml) lime juice

Salt and pepper

¼ tsp ground cumin

1 CUP (100 G) CUCUMBER

1 cup (60 g) radish greens

½ OF A BUNCH OF CILANTRO

1 avocado

1¼ CUPS (150 G) FENNEL

4 radishes

Bombay Bowl

Are you interested in a few spoonfuls of Ayurvedic Medicine? Cardamom and saffron are great for the stomach, and together with cashews and sweet mango, and a colorful mix of fruit on top, its guaranteed to lift any mood.

Toppings

1/2 cup (100 g) papaya, cut into small cubes

2 tbsp (22 g) pomegranate seeds

1 tbsp (5 g) shredded coconut

⅓ cup
(50 g)
cashews
(soaked overnight in water)

One small

mango

A DASH OF LIME JUICE

1/4 tsp
saffran powder

one banana

1 PINCH OF GROUND
CARDAMOM

Golden Fall

Here's how you defy the increasing chill of the fall weather and the inevitable case of the sniffles. This super colorful vegetable and fruit mix will help strengthen your immune system. Now let the winter come; you'll be ready.

Toppings

1 blood orange

2 tbsp (13 g) coarsely chopped almonds

1 tbsp (7 g) coarsely chopped pecans

1 tbsp (8 g) coarsely chopped pistachios

1 cup
(100 g)

1 really ripe
persimmon

parsnip

JUICE OF ONE
orange

2 TBSP (28 G)
SEA BUCKTHORN
PUREE
↓

3 Jerusalem artichokes,
(about ¾ cup, or 120 g)

1 PINCH OF
GROUND CINNAMON

ABOUT THE AUTHORS

IRINA PAWASSAR has been making smoothies for family and friends for years and often holds smoothie workshops. She completed an apprenticeship to become a Raw Food Chef in the U.S. and has prepared raw foods at several seminars in Ireland. She has inspired many with her passion for simple but super healthy foods. As head chef at the Munich-based restaurant Gratitude, she created many colorful smoothies and always found a way to add the all-important chlorophyll. She hasn't had the flu in six years.

TANJA DUSY feels most comfortable when it is really busy in the kitchen. She has worked many years as cookbook editor and also made a name for herself as author. Her book *Smoothie: Fruit Power in a Jar* has sold 120,000 copies and is considered a bestseller among smoothie books. As a kitchen professional, Dusy develops recipes that are not only reliable, but also have that something extra. Again, with *Smoothie Power*, she proves just how easy it is to combine healthy food and great taste.

INDEX

A

acai berry
Bloody Hell, 50–51
Blue Velvet, 164–165
introduction to, 8
A-Game, 58–59
agave nectar
Blue Velvet, 164–165
Choco Shock, 162–163
Green Machine, 80–81
Mexican Mango, 64–65
Peppy Paprika,
148–149
White Star, 138–139
almond cream
Cherry Kiss, 166–167
Peaches & Cream,
140–141
almond milk
Big Fig, 120–121
Blueberry Dream,
42–43
Cacao Smoothie, 48–49
Chai Smoothie, 46–47
Cherry Kiss, 166–167
Chocorangina, 122–123
Gold Milk, 30–31
Mexican Mango, 64–65
Mister Muesli,
168–169
Pink Milk, 100–101
Pink Power, 34–35
Pinky Pie, 160–161
almonds
Big Fig, 120–121

Cherry Kiss, 166–167
Golden Fall, 176–177
Peaches & Cream,
140–141
Pinky Pie, 160–161
Always Full, 60–61
Always-Works-Super-
Crunchy-Granola
Pink Elephant, 142–143
recipe, 7
amaranth
Cherry Kiss, 166–167
Indian Summer,
144–145
Pea for Tea, 152–153
apples
A-Game, 58–59
Arugula Rocket, 88–89
Banana Joe, 98–99
Brocco Lilly, 128–129
Fit Kid, 134–135
Flu Shake, 114–115
Goji-Queen/Aronia-
Queen, 18–19
Green Princess,
170–171
Indian Summer,
144–145
Low Carb, 32–33
MacCucumber,
106–107
Mean Green Smoothie,
40–41
Mister Muesli, 168–169
Par & Sley, 12–13
Pea for Tea, 152–153

Total Local Winter
Smoothie, 38–39
apricots
Road Drink, 66–67
Wild Child, 70–71
aronia berries
Goji-Queen/Aronia-
Queen, 18–19
Total Local Winter
Smoothie, 38–39
artichokes, in Golden
Fall, 176–177
arugula
Arugula Rocket, 88–89
Rock It Baby, 56–57
avocados
A-Game, 58–59
Always Full, 60–61
Bro-Juice, 92–93
Evergreen, 172–173
Green Oasis, 150–151
Hangover Cure, 44–45
Kale Rider, 28–29
Pink Salad, 156–157
Pinky Pie, 160–161
Road Drink, 66–67
Sexy Thing, 62–63

B

bananas
Arugula Rocket, 88–89
Banana Coco Joe,
116–117
Banana Joe, 98–99
Big Fig, 120–121

Bloody & Berry, 54–55
Blueberry Dream,
42–43
Blue Velvet, 164–165
Bombay Bowl, 174–175
Brocco Lilly, 128–129
Cherry Kiss, 166–167
Choco Shock, 162–163
Dragon Juice, 104–105
Goji-Queen/Aronia-
Queen, 18–19
Green Limo, 124–125
Green Princess,
170–171
Halloween Smoothie,
22–23
Hangover Cure, 44–45
Hello, Charlie Brown!,
146–147
Island in the Sun,
158–159
Johnny Blue, 102–103
Jonny Kale, 16–17
KaCo, 130–131
King Louie, 24–25
Magic Manni, 86–87
Mean Green Smoothie,
40–41
Mellow Yellow, 154–155
Mister Muesli, 168–169
Mr. Strawberry, 96–97
Pea for Tea, 152–153
Peppy Paprika,
148–149
Pineapple Express,
72–73

Pink Elephant, 142–143
Rock It Baby, 56–57
South Pacific Dream,
110–111
Tropical Smoothie,
36–37
White Star, 138–139
Wild Child, 70–71
basil
Bloody & Berry, 54–55
Green Princess,
170–171
beets
Bloody Hell, 50–51
Hello, Charlie Brown!,
146–147
Indian Summer,
144–145
Pink Milk, 100–101
Pink Power, 34–35
Raspberry Dragon,
112–113
Total Local Winter
Smoothie, 38–39
Big Fig, 120–121
blackberries
Blue Velvet, 164–165
Peaches & Cream,
140–141
Pink Elephant, 142–143
Total Local Winter
Smoothie, 38–39
blenders, 5
blood oranges, in Golden
Fall, 176–177
Bloody & Berry, 54–55
Bloody Hell, 50–51
blossoms
Indian Summer,
144–145
introduction to, 9
blueberries
Blueberry Dream,
42–43
Blue Velvet, 164–165
Johnny Blue, 102–103
Mister Muesli, 168–169
Pink Elephant, 142–143
Pink Salad, 156–157
Blue Velvet, 164–165
Bombay Bowl, 174–175
Brazil nuts
Cacao Smoothie, 48–49
DaNuMi, 126–127
broccoli
Brocco Lilly, 128–129
Bro-Juice, 92–93

Par & Sley, 12–13
Bro-Juice, 92–93

C
cabbage
Always Full, 60–61
KaCo, 130–131
Kale Rider, 28–29
cacao
Cherry Kiss, 166–167
Chocorangina, 122–123
Choco Shock, 162–163
introduction to, 8
King Louie, 24–25
Mr. Strawberry, 96–97
Pea for Tea, 152–153
Pink Power, 34–35
White Star, 138–139
cacao powder
Cacao Smoothie, 48–49
Chocorangina, 122–123
King Louie, 24–25
cardamom
Bloody & Berry, 54–55
Bombay Bowl, 174–175
Chai Smoothie, 46–47
Halloween Smoothie,
22–23
Hello, Charlie Brown!,
146–147
introduction to, 8
cashews, in Bombay
Bowl, 174–175
celery
Fit Kid, 134–135
Green Machine, 80–81
Mellow Yellow,
154–155
Par & Sley, 12–13
Chai Smoothie, 46–47
chard, in Magic Manni,
86–87
cherries
Blue Velvet, 164–165
Cherry Kiss, 166–167
Peppy Paprika,
148–149
chia seeds
A-Game, 58–59
Brocco Lilly, 128–129
Fit Kid, 134–135
Green Princess,
170–171
Hangover Cure, 44–45
introduction to, 8
King Louie, 24–25

Magic Manni, 86–87
Mean Green Smoothie,
40–41
Peppy Paprika,
148–149
Pink Salad, 156–157
Princess Melonie,
108–109
Raspberry Dragon,
112–113
White Star, 138–139
Wild Child, 70–71
chile peppers
Goa Beach, 90–91
Peppy Paprika,
148–149
Chocorangina, 122–123
Choco Shock, 162–163
cilantro
Evergreen, 172–173
Sexy Thing, 62–63
Tropical Smoothie,
36–37
cinnamon
Big Fig, 120–121
Chai Smoothie, 46–47
Choco Shock, 162–163
DaNuMi, 126–127
Golden Fall, 176–177
Indian Summer,
144–145
Mister Muesli, 168–169
coconut
Always-Works-Super-
Crunchy-Granola, 7
Banana Coco Joe,
116–117
Blueberry Dream,
42–43
Bombay Bowl, 174–175
Goa Beach, 90–91
Green Oasis, 150–151
introduction to, 9
King Louie, 24–25
Peppy Paprika,
148–149
Sexy Thing, 62–63
South Pacific Dream,
110–111
Tropical Smoothie,
36–37
White Star, 138–139
coconut milk, in Green
Oasis, 150–151
coconut sugar
Always Full, 60–61
Brocco Lilly, 128–129

Chocorangina, 122–123
Green Lemonade,
74–75
Johnny Blue, 102–103
MacCucumber,
106–107
Pink Milk, 100–101
Raspberry Dragon,
112–113
Rock It Baby, 56–57
coconut water
Hangover Cure, 44–45
introduction to, 9
KaCo, 130–131
Kale Rider, 28–29
King Louie, 24–25
Tropical Smoothie,
36–37
coconut yogurt
Island in the Sun,
158–159
Pink Elephant, 142–143
cranberries
Always-Works-Super-
Crunchy-Granola, 7
Choco Shock, 162–163
Indian Summer,
144–145
Mellow Yellow, 154–155
cucumber
Evergreen, 172–173
Green Lemonade,
74–75
Green Machine, 80–81
MacCucumber,
106–107
Mean Green Smoothie,
40–41
Par & Sley, 12–13
currants, in Hello,
Charlie Brown!,
146–147

D
dandelion greens
Garden Dream, 68–69
introduction to, 9
Johnny Blue, 102–103
DaNuMi, 126–127
dates
A-Game, 58–59
Banana Coco Joe,
116–117
DaNuMi, 126–127
Dragon Juice, 104–105
Garden Dream, 68–69

Gold Milk, 30–31
Green Limo, 124–125
Green Oasis, 150–151
Happy Pear, 84–85
KaCo, 130–131
Pineapple Express,
72–73
Smoothie Mediterra-
nean, 26–27
White Star, 138–139
Dragon Juice, 104–105

E

Evergreen, 172–173

F

fennel
Evergreen, 172–173
Iron King, 78–79
Mango to Tango, 14–15
figs
Big Fig, 120–121
Smoothie Mediterra-
nean, 26–27
Fit Kid, 134–135
five grain flakes
Mister Muesli, 168–169
Peaches & Cream,
140–141
flaxseed
Always-Works-Super-
Crunchy-Granola, 7
Bloody Hell, 50–51
Chocorangina,
122–123
Dragon Juice, 104–105
introduction to, 9
Mean Green Smoothie,
40–41
Mister Muesli, 168–169
Power Bomb, 82–83
Flu Shake, 114–115

G

Garden Dream, 68–69
ginger
Always-Works-Super-
Crunchy-Granola, 7
Bro-Juice, 92–93
Chai Smoothie, 46–47
Flu Shake, 114–115
Gold Milk, 30–31
Green Machine, 80–81
introduction to, 8

Low Carb, 32–33
Mean Green Smoothie,
40–41
Goa Beach, 90–91
goji berries
Always-Works-Super-
Crunchy-Granola, 7
Goji-Queen/Aronia-
Queen, 18–19
Green Princess,
170–171
introduction to, 9
Mango Mandy, 132–133
Raspberry Dragon,
112–113
Golden Fall, 176–177
Gold Milk, 30–31
granola
Always-Works-Super-
Crunchy-Granola, 7
Mister Muesli, 168–169
Pink Elephant, 142–143
grapes
A-Game, 58–59
Bloody Hell, 50–51
Hangover Cure, 44–45
Indian Summer,
144–145
Low Carb, 32–33
Magic Manni, 86–87
Mexican Mango, 64–65
Pink Salad, 156–157
Green Lemonade, 74–75
Green Limo, 124–125
Green Machine, 80–81
Green Mouse, 118–119
Green Oasis, 150–151
Green Princess, 170–171
ground cherries, in
Peppy Paprika, 148–149
ground elder
Dragon Juice, 104–105
introduction to, 9
Wild Child, 70–71

H

Halloween Smoothie,
22–23
Hangover Cure, 44–45
Happy Pear, 84–85
hazelnut milk
Choco Shock, 162–163
Indian Summer,
144–145
hazelnuts
Cacao Smoothie, 48–49

Choco Shock, 162–163
DaNuMi, 126–127
Indian Summer,
144–145
Mister Muesli, 168–169
Hello, Charlie Brown!,
146–147
hemp
Happy Pear, 84–85
Mean Green Smoothie,
40–41
Total Local Winter
Smoothie, 38–39
hemp powder
introduction to, 8
Pineapple Express,
72–73
Total Local Winter
Smoothie, 38–39
hemp seeds
Always-Works-Super-
Crunchy-Granola, 7
Banana Coco Joe,
116–117
Chocorangina, 122–123
DaNuMi, 126–127
Green Mouse, 118–119
Happy Pear, 84–85
introduction to, 8
Pink Milk, 100–101
honey
Always-Works-Super-
Crunchy-Granola, 7
Cacao Smoothie, 48–49
Chai Smoothie, 46–47
Flu Shake, 114–115
Goji-Queen/Aronia-
Queen, 18–19
Halloween Smoothie,
22–23
Par & Sley, 12–13
Peaches & Cream,
140–141
Pink Elephant, 142–143
Pink Power, 34–35
Pinky Pie, 160–161
honeydew melon, in
Honey & Tini, 76–77

I

immersion blenders, 5
Indian Summer, 144–145
Iron King, 78–79
Island in the Sun, 158–159

J

Johnny Blue, 102–103
Jonny Kale, 16–17

K

KaCo, 130–131
kale
Always Full, 60–61
Green Oasis, 150–151
Hangover Cure, 44–45
introduction to, 9
Jonny Kale, 16–17
KaCo, 130–131
Kale Rider, 28–29
Mean Green Smoothie,
40–41
Power Bomb, 82–83
Total Local Winter
Smoothie, 38–39
King Louie, 24–25
kiwi
Always Full, 60–61
Banana Joe, 98–99
Flu Shake, 114–115
Green Mouse, 118–119
Green Princess,
170–171
Hello, Charlie Brown!,
146–147
Mellow Yellow, 154–155
Pea for Tea, 152–153

L

lemongrass, in Island in
the Sun, 158–159
lemon juice
Bloody Hell, 50–51
Bro-Juice, 92–93
Flu Shake, 114–115
Green Lemonade,
74–75
Green Limo, 124–125
Green Princess,
170–171
Honey & Tini, 76–77
Low Carb, 32–33
MacCucumber,
106–107
Mister Muesli, 168–169
Peppy Paprika,
148–149
Princess Melonie,
108–109
Smoothie Mediterra-
nean, 26–27

South Pacific Dream,
110–111
lemon slices, in Green
Machine, 80–81
lettuce
Green Limo, 124–125
Mean Green Smoothie,
40–41
Pink Salad, 156–157
lime juice
Bombay Bowl, 174–175
Evergreen, 172–173
Goa Beach, 90–91
Green Lemonade,
74–75
Hello, Charlie Brown!,
146–147
Island in the Sun,
158–159
Kale Rider, 28–29
Pink Salad, 156–157
Pinky Pie, 160–161
South Pacific Dream,
110–111
Summer Dream, 20–21
Tropical Smoothie,
36–37
Low Carb, 32–33

M
macadamia nut milk, in
King Louie, 24–25
maca powder
introduction to, 8
Mean Green Smoothie,
40–41
MacCucumber, 106–107
Magic Manni, 86–87
mangoes
Bombay Bowl, 174–175
Green Machine, 80–81
Hangover Cure, 44–45
Hello, Charlie Brown!,
146–147
Island in the Sun,
158–159
Mango Mandy, 132–133
Mango to Tango, 14–15
Mellow Yellow, 154–155
Mexican Mango, 64–65
Peaches & Cream,
140–141
Peppy Paprika,
148–149
Power Bomb, 82–83

South Pacific Dream,
110–111
maple syrup
Always-Works-Super-
Crunchy-Granola, 7
Cacao Smoothie, 48–49
Chai Smoothie, 46–47
Goji-Queen/Aronia-
Queen, 18–19
Gold Milk, 30–31
Halloween Smoothie,
22–23
Indian Summer,
144–145
Peaches & Cream,
140–141
Pink Power, 34–35
Pinky Pie, 160–161
Mean Green Smoothie,
40–41
melba toast, in Pinky Pie,
160–161
Mellow Yellow, 154–155
Mexican Mango, 64–65
mint
Bloody Hell, 50–51
Cacao Smoothie, 48–49
Garden Dream, 68–69
Goa Beach, 90–91
Green Lemonade,
74–75
Honey & Tini, 76–77
Island in the Sun,
158–159
MacCucumber,
106–107
Mr. Strawberry, 96–97
Par & Sley, 12–13
Pea for Tea, 152–153
Pink Elephant, 142–143
Pink Power, 34–35
Princess Melonie,
108–109
Summer Dream,
20–21
Mister Muesli, 168–169
Mr. Strawberry, 96–97
muesli
Mister Muesli, 168–169
Pineapple Express,
72–73
mulberries, in Blue
Velvet, 164–165

N
nectarines, in Peaches &
Cream, 140–141
nettle
Banana Joe, 98–99
introduction to, 9
Road Drink, 66–67
nutmeg, in Chai
Smoothie, 46–47

O
oat milk
Chocorangina, 122–123
DaNuMi, 126–127
Pineapple Express,
72–73
Pink Milk, 100–101
oats
King Louie, 24–25
White Star, 138–139
oranges
Bro-Juice, 92–93
Golden Fall, 176–177
Halloween Smoothie,
22–23
Iron King, 78–79
Jonny Kale, 16–17
Rock It Baby, 56–57
orange juice
Bloody Hell, 50–51
Blue Velvet, 164–165
Chocorangina, 122–123
Fit Kid, 134–135
Flu Shake, 114–115
Golden Fall, 176–177
Halloween Smoothie,
22–23
Mango to Tango, 14–15
Mellow Yellow, 154–155
Peaches & Cream,
140–141
orange peppers, in
Peppy Paprika, 148–149

P
papaya
Bombay Bowl, 174–175
Goa Beach, 90–91
Hello, Charlie Brown!,
146–147
Tropical Smoothie,
36–37
parsley
Fit Kid, 134–135
Green Machine, 80–81

Happy Pear, 84–85
Iron King, 78–79
Low Carb, 32–33
Par & Sley, 12–13
parsnips
Golden Fall, 176–177
Mister Muesli, 168–169
passion fruit
Island in the Sun,
158–159
Tropical Smoothie,
36–37
peaches
Peaches & Cream,
140–141
Road Drink, 66–67
Peaches & Cream,
140–141
Pea for Tea, 152–153
peanuts
Hello, Charlie Brown!,
146–147
Mellow Yellow, 154–155
pears
Always Full, 60–61
Choco Shock, 162–163
Happy Pear, 84–85
KaCo, 130–131
peas, in Pea for Tea,
152–153
pecans
Golden Fall, 176–177
Green Oasis, 150–151
Peppy Paprika, 148–149
persimmon
Golden Fall, 176–177
Peppy Paprika,
148–149
pineapple
Green Mouse, 118–119
Green Oasis, 150–151
Kale Rider, 28–29
Mellow Yellow, 154–155
Pineapple Express,
72–73
Sexy Thing, 62–63
Tropical Smoothie,
36–37
White Star, 138–139
Pink Elephant, 142–143
Pink Milk, 100–101
Pink Power, 34–35
Pink Salad, 156–157
Pinky Pie, 160–161
pistachios
Golden Fall, 176–177

Peaches & Cream,
140–141
Pinky Pie, 160–161
plums, in Indian
Summer, 144–145
pomegranate seeds
Blue Velvet, 164–165
Bombay Bowl, 174–175
Green Oasis, 150–151
Smoothie Mediterra-
nean, 26–27
Power Bomb, 82–83
Princess Melonie,
108–109
pumpkin, in Halloween
Smoothie, 22–23

Q

quinoa
Cherry Kiss, 166–167
Indian Summer,
144–145

R

radishes, in Evergreen,
172–173
raisins, in Mister Muesli,
168–169
raspberries
Blue Velvet, 164–165
Garden Dream, 68–69
Pink Elephant, 142–143
Pink Salad, 156–157
Pinky Pie, 160–161
Raspberry Dragon,
112–113
Rice and Coconut Drink
A-Game, 58–59
Banana Coco Joe,
116–117
Jonny Kale, 16–17
White Star, 138–139
rice milk
Hangover Cure, 44–45
Pink Power, 34–35
Road Drink, 66–67
Rock It Baby, 56–57
rose blossom, in Pink
Milk, 100–101

S

saffran powder, in Bom-
bay Bowl, 174–175
sea buckthorn, in Golden
Fall, 176–177

sesame seeds
Always-Works-Super-
Crunchy-Granola, 7
Green Princess,
170–171
Hello, Charlie Brown!,
146–147
Sexy Thing, 62–63
Sexy Thing, 62–63
Smoothie Mediterra-
nean, 26–27
South Pacific Dream,
110–111
spinach
A-Game, 58–59
Green Limo, 124–125
Green Mouse, 118–119
Green Princess,
170–171
Low Carb, 32–33
Mexican Mango, 64–65
Pineapple Express,
72–73
South Pacific Dream,
110–111
spirulina
introduction to, 8
Par & Sley, 12–13
Road Drink, 66–67
sprouts
Evergreen, 172–173
Total Local Winter
Smoothie, 38–39
stevia
introduction to, 8
Par & Sley, 12–13
stinging nettles
Banana Joe, 98–99
introduction to, 9
Road Drink, 66–67
strawberries
Bloody & Berry, 54–55
Island in the Sun,
158–159
Mr. Strawberry, 96–97
Pink Elephant, 142–143
Pink Salad, 156–157
Pinky Pie, 160–161
Summer Dream, 20–21
sunflower seeds
Always-Works-Super-
Crunchy-Granola, 7
Pink Salad, 156–157
Super Danke shop, 5

T

tangerines, in Mango
Mandy, 132–133
tomatoes, in Evergreen,
172–173
topinambur, in Total
Local Winter Smoothie,
38–39
Tropical Smoothie, 36–37
turmeric, in Gold Milk,
30–31

V

vanilla
Blueberry Dream,
42–43
Blue Velvet, 164–165
Cacao Smoothie, 48–49
Chai Smoothie, 46–47
Cherry Kiss, 166–167
Goji-Queen/Aronia-
Queen, 18–19
Pinky Pie, 160–161
White Star, 138–139

W

walnut milk, in Arugula
Rocket, 88–89
walnuts, in DaNuMi,
126–127
watermelon
Princess Melonie,
108–109
Summer Dream, 20–21
White Star, 138–139
Wild Child, 70–71

X

xylitol
Always Full, 60–61
Brocco Lilly, 128–129
Chocorangina,
122–123
Green Lemonade,
74–75
MacCucumber,
106–107
Pink Milk, 100–101
Raspberry Dragon,
112–113

Y

yellow peppers, in Low

Carb, 32–33
yogurt
Island in the Sun,
158–159
Pink Elephant,
142–143